Charles Dickens

Paul Shipton

Level 3

Series Editors: Andy Hopkins and Jocelyn Potter

Pearson Education Limited

Edinburgh Gate, Harlow,
Essex CM20 2JE, England
and Associated Companies throughout the world.

Pack ISBN: 978-1-4058-5211-1
Book ISBN: 978-1-4058-5065-0
CD-ROM ISBN: 978-1-4058-5066-7

This edition first published by Pearson Education Ltd 2007

3 5 7 9 10 8 6 4 2

Text copyright © Paul Shipton 2007
Illustrations by Julián Totino Tedesco

Set in 11/13pt A. Garamond
Printed in China
SWTC/02

Produced for the Publishers by AC Estudio Editorial S.L.

Published by Pearson Education Ltd in association with Penguin Books Ltd,
both companies being subsidiaries of Pearson Plc

Acknowledgements
We are grateful to the following for permission to reproduce photographs:

Aquarius Collection: page 12, page 55; **Bridgeman Art Library:** page 36; **Charles Dickens Museum,
London:** page 3, page 10, page 16, page 20, page 21, page 37, page 40, page 44, page 54;
Getty Images: page 1; **Mary Evans Picture Library:** page 6, page 52; **Ronald Grant Archive:** page 45

Picture research by Frances Topp

Every effort has been made to trace the copyright holders and we apologise in advance for any
unintentional omissions. We would be pleased to insert the appropriate
acknowledgement in any subsequent edition of this publication.

For a complete list of the titles available in the Penguin Active Reading series please write to your local
Pearson Longman office or to: Penguin Readers Marketing Department, Pearson Education,
Edinburgh Gate, Harlow, Essex CM20 2JE, England.

Contents

1.1 What's the book about?

1 What books by Charles Dickens do you know? Put the letters next to the book titles.

    a I have heard of the book.
    b I have read the book.
    c I have seen a film of the book.
    d I haven't heard of it.

Can you add other books to the list?

Oliver Twist	
A Christmas Carol	
David Copperfield	
Great Expectations	

2 Talk to another student who knows the same story as you. What is the story about? What did you like about it? What did it tell you about life in the writer's time?

1.2 What happens first?

Look at the words in *italics* on pages 1 and 5 and the pictures in Chapters 1 and 2. What do you think? Write the correct words in the sentences.

1   Charles Dickens was born in the ....

1700s	1800s	1900s

2   Dickens was born in ....

England	the US	Ireland

3   Dickens's parents had problems with ....

their marriage	money	their children

4   When he was young, Dickens had to work in ....

a school	a prison	a factory

5   Dickens's first book was mostly about ....

London	country life	rich people

CHAPTER 1

The School of Life

Suddenly life became harder. For the first time,
Charles began to understand the family's money problems.

Charles Dickens was forty-three in February, 1855. After a birthday dinner with friends, he decided to walk home through the snow. His walk took him past a large house called Gad's Hill Place. Dickens knew this house from years before. When he was only a boy, he walked past the same house, near Chatham in the south of England, with his father. Now the adult Dickens remembered his father's words: 'If you work hard, one day you can live in a house like that.' To the young boy, the big, expensive house seemed like a dream.

But Dickens *did* work very hard and now he was rich and famous; he was the most popular writer in Britain. He decided something that cold February night – to buy Gad's Hill Place. Two years later, Dickens and his family moved in to the house. The young boy's dream was now real.

Not all of Dickens's memories of his early life were happy. Those years were often hard, but they helped to shape the adult writer.

Charles John Huffam Dickens was born in 1812 near Portsmouth on the south coast of England. His father, John, worked in an office. It was not a bad job, but John had a terrible weakness. He liked to spend more than he earned.

The Dickens family never stayed in one place for very long. Sometimes they left because John Dickens was not able to pay his **debt**s. The family's money problems were made worse by the number of children. Charles had one older sister, Fanny. After Charles was born, his parents had six more children. There were six more mouths to feed.

Charles Dickens in his 40s

debt /det/ (n) borrowed money that you must pay back

Charles was five when the family moved to Chatham, a busy town on the coast. This was the happiest time for him. His father had a new job and the family was able to live comfortably in a nice house. Charles loved to walk around the town with his father. The family were able to pay someone to look after the children now. Charles loved to hear stories from their nurse, Mary Weller. She did not always tell the young boy pleasant stories; Mary preferred stories of blood and murder! Much later, Dickens thought that his interest in the darker side of life came from his nurse and her stories.

Charles's mother, Elizabeth, taught him to read. Then he and his sister Fanny were sent to a local 'school' – a room over a shop where an old lady taught a few children reading and writing. Charles was small and often ill, so he could not always play outside with other children. Soon he was reading as many books as he could. He also began to write his own stories. Sometimes his parents took him to the theatre. The boy lived in a world of stories, and he loved them all.

But John Dickens's money problems did not go away. In the Chatham years, he continued to spend too much and often borrowed money from friends or relatives. In 1821 the family moved to a smaller house. Then John Dickens's job was moved to London, and he was paid less money. At the age of ten, Charles moved with his family into a small house in Camden Town, just outside the city of London.

Suddenly life became harder. For the first time, Charles began to understand the family's money problems. Sometimes they had to sell their furniture, clothes and even books. They had no money to send Charles to school now. But they continued to send his sister Fanny to an expensive school.

With much more free time, Charles began to walk alone through the streets of London and by the River Thames. This was a time of great change in Britain.

New factories, railways and machines were changing British life for ever. The old ways were disappearing fast. More and more people were moving from the country to the cities for work. London was soon the biggest city in the world, but life was not easy for the poor there. They worked long hours in dangerous jobs at the new factories. Often more than one family lived in the same small house. Some people had no home or food; they lived on the streets and asked strangers for food or money. Some of them stole. The city was a strange, new world for young Charles. He often returned to this world in his **novel**s.

At home, the Dickens family's money problems grew worse and worse. Charles's mother Elizabeth tried to earn some money by opening a school. Not one pupil came and the school failed.

novel /ˈnɒvəl/ (n) a long, written story

At this time, a friend of the family, John Lamert, suggested a new idea. Lamert worked in a factory where black boot **polish** was made. He offered Charles a job at the factory. And so, two days after his twelfth birthday, Charles started work at a dirty, old factory by the river.

Six days a week, he walked more than five kilometres to reach the factory. Then he worked for ten and a half boring hours, putting the company's name on pots of boot polish. It was not unusual for children to have jobs like this in the 1820s. But Charles had bigger hopes for his future. The other boys were poor and most of them could not read. Some were **orphan**s. They were kind to Dickens, but he hated every second of the job. He knew that he was different from the others.

This picture from Life of Dickens *by the writer's friend John Forster shows Dickens's feelings about the boot polish factory.*

What's in a name?

Charles's best friend at the factory was an older boy called Bob Fagin. When Charles was ill at the factory, Fagin helped him. Later Dickens used the name Fagin for one of the **character**s in *Oliver Twist*. In that novel, Fagin taught children to become street thieves. Perhaps Dickens used the name for this character because his time at the factory was one of his worst memories.

Ten days after Charles began this job, his father was sent to Marshalsea Prison, south of the River Thames. This was a special prison for people who could not pay their debts. It was different from other prisons – John Dickens continued

polish /'pɒlɪʃ/ (n) something used to shine shoes
orphan /'ɔːfən/ (n) a child whose parents are dead
character /'kærɪktə/ (n) a fictional person in a book, play or film

to work and receive money. His family were able to live with him in the prison. Elizabeth and the younger children lived there, but not Charles. Now he was really alone. He found a room in a house and continued to work at the factory. Every evening he bought dinner with his own money and then walked back to his room. By the end of the week, he often had no money for food. He visited the prison most days. The prison **scene**s in many of Dickens's novels seem real because young Charles knew prisons very well.

After a few months, Charles's grandmother died. She left John Dickens enough money to pay his debts. The family left the prison, but Charles was still not free. His mother wanted him to continue at the factory, and Dickens never forgave her for that.

John Dickens saved the boy now. With more money in his pocket again, he decided that Charles must return to school. The boy was sent to a school in North London called Wellington Academy. This was very different from modern schools; there were two hundred boys of all ages in one big classroom. The teachers were quick to hit their pupils. Dickens later compared some schools to prisons.

But, after his months at the boot polish factory, Dickens was happy at school. He and his group of friends wrote and acted in plays. They wrote stories, poems and jokes, and they put them in a school magazine called *Our Newspaper*. Dickens did not tell his new friends about his past life at the factory. He was again in his world of stories.

There was only enough money for Dickens to be at school for two years. Then, soon after his fifteenth birthday, he left and began to look for work.

scene /siːn/ (n) a short part of a book, play or film

CHAPTER 2

First Success

Each of these short reports showed a side of life in London
– on the streets, in the bars, in the courts and prisons.

At this time, London was the business centre of the world. Because of this, there were thousands of office workers in the city. Dickens's job was in an office too. He worked for a **lawyer** and the job was boring to the sixteen-year-old. In his opinion, the only purpose of the law was 'to make money for itself'.

But with more money now, Dickens could continue to enjoy London life. He loved going to the theatre, but he also liked to watch people in the streets. He listened to their conversations and noticed everything about them.

At seventeen, he got a new job as a newspaper reporter. He sat in law courts and took notes. His opinion of the law did not get any better. He thought that the judges were old and silly. Soon he moved to another reporting job. From 1831 to 1834, he listened to and reported the speeches of politicians in parliament. He learned a lot about the changes in the country during this time. Politicians passed laws about the poor, about schools and about the new factories. For the rest of his life, Dickens did not stop working to help the country's poor.

But another great interest still burned in his heart – theatre. In fact, in 1832 he almost became a professional actor. There was a possible part for him in a play in a London theatre. But Dickens was ill and he did not go to the theatre.

At about this time, Dickens fell in love. The girl's name was Maria Beadnell and she was the daughter of rich parents. Dickens later described her as 'everything that everybody ever wanted'. He wrote long letters telling her about his love. On some nights he stood outside her house and watched her bedroom window. But Maria did not return his love. Her parents knew about John Dickens's time in prison. In their opinion, Dickens was not good enough for their daughter.

Dickens's heart was broken, but he worked harder than ever. In 1832 he got a job on a new newspaper. The next year, he started working at a bigger newspaper. He went to meetings around the country and reported them to his readers.

Dickens also began different kinds of writing. In 1833 he wrote a short, funny story about a London family. Nervously, he posted it to a magazine. He did not hear from them. But there was a wonderful surprise when he bought the next copy of the magazine. His story was in it! He was not yet twenty-two and he was a **publish**ed writer.

---

lawyer /ˈlɔːjə/ (n) someone who helps people understand the law. *Lawyers* also speak for people in law courts.
publish /ˈpʌblɪʃ/ (v) to print a book, magazine or newspaper and sell it

Pictures by George Cruikshank added to the success of Sketches by Boz.

Dickens began to write more and more for the magazine. Each of these short reports showed a side of life in London – on the streets, in the bars, in the courts and prisons. Many of them were funny, but some could bring tears to the reader's eye. With great skill, his words gave readers a look into other people's lives.

Dickens wrote these stories under the name 'Boz', and they were soon very popular. A publisher, John Macrone, decided to put the work into a book. And so, in February 1836, readers could buy *Sketches by Boz*, Charles Dickens's first book. It was an immediate success.

George Hogarth, a writer and **editor** for an evening newspaper, liked the book very much. His three daughters all liked the hard-working and successful young writer and Dickens became close to the family. In 1835 he asked the oldest sister, Catherine, to marry him. He was still working as a reporter, and he was very busy. Catherine was a kind and quiet woman. Sometimes she became impatient that he was always working. Dickens's love for Catherine was not like his love for Maria Beadnell. He wanted a happy, family life, but his work came first now. The two were not married until the following year.

Dickens was asked to write a new book, about life in the country. At this time, most novels came out in three parts. The publishers Chapman & Hall had a new idea: they wanted to publish Dickens's next book in twenty parts. Each month, readers could buy a part of the novel in a magazine for a small amount of money. This meant that a lot more people could buy books.

Still using the name 'Boz', Dickens wrote about a group of friends. There were a lot of characters in the novel, but readers really loved two of them – Mr Pickwick and Sam Weller.

Great Dickens Characters: Sam Weller

Sam Weller was the most popular character in *The Pickwick Papers*. He works for Pickwick, but he often knows much more than Pickwick. Readers loved

edit /'edɪt/ (v) to make changes to another person's writing before it is printed

Sam Weller usually knows best.

Sam's way of saying things – there were even Sam Weller joke books! It is interesting that Dickens gave this character the last name of his nurse from many years before.

In the novel, Dickens offered readers the pleasant world of a disappearing England. Much of the book was light and funny, but he also added darker scenes. In one part of the story, Pickwick goes to prison because he has not paid a debt. It is clear where Dickens got the idea.

After a slow start, the magazine of *Pickwick Papers* finally sold 40,000 copies every month, ending in November, 1837. Dickens was popular and famous, but that was just the beginning. He wrote two short plays for the theatre. His work as a reporter ended, but he agreed to be the editor of a new magazine. Dickens continued to work as an editor for most of his life. But even before the last part of *Pickwick Papers* was published, he started a new novel. Like *Pickwick Papers*, a new part came out every month. But the funny stories about Pickwick and his friends did not prepare readers for the serious side of *Oliver Twist*.

2.1 Were you right?

Look back at your answers to Activity 1.2 on page iv. Then read the sentences. Are they true (✓) or untrue (✗)? Write the untrue sentences correctly below.

1 ☐ Charles Dickens was born in the south of England.

2 ☐ Dickens was born in the late 1700s.

3 ☐ His mother liked to spend more than she earned.

4 ☐ Dickens's father was sent to prison while Charles was working in a factory.

5 ☐ *Pickwick Papers* was a book of Dickens's short writings about life in London.

....

....

....

2.2 What more did you learn?

In what order did these happen? Number the sentences, 1–10.

a ☐ Dickens worked in a lawyer's office.

b ☐ He fell in love with Maria Beadnell.

c ☐1☐ The Dickens family moved to London.

d ☐ Dickens married Catherine Hogarth.

e ☐ John Dickens was sent to prison.

f ☐ The final part of *Pickwick Papers* was published.

g ☐ Dickens went to school at Wellington Academy.

h ☐ Dickens got a job as a newspaper reporter.

i ☐ He became a published writer.

j ☐ Dickens had to work in a factory.

2.3 Language in use

Look at the sentences on the right. Then finish the sentences below in the same way.

> Lamert worked in a factory where black boot polish **was made.** The family's problems **were made** worse by the number of children.

1 Dickens ....was taught........ (teach) to read by his mother.

2 John Dickens's job .... (move) to London.

3 Dickens's father .... (send) to prison.

4 Children .... (use) for factory work.

5 Dickens's heart .... (break) when Maria did not return his love.

6 40,000 copies of *Pickwick Papers* .... (sell) every month.

2.4 What's next?

Look at the pictures on pages 11 and 12. What do you think Dickens's next novel, *Oliver Twist*, is about? Circle the correct answers.

1 Oliver Twist lives

    a in a school.
    b with his parents.
    c in a special home for poor people.

2 The man in the picture on page 11 is angry because

    a Oliver steals food.
    b Oliver asks for more food.
    c Oliver does not eat all his food.

3 Oliver runs away to London and meets Fagin. Fagin

    a steals from him.
    b wants to prepare him for a life of crime.
    c takes Oliver to the police.

4 With this novel Dickens wanted

    a to make the lives of poor people better.
    b to describe the lives of factory workers.
    c to suggest more time in prison for street criminals.

CHAPTER 3

In the Workhouse

*Dickens wanted his readers to be angry about
the terrible conditions for poor children like Oliver Twist.*

In his private life, Charles was happily
married to Catherine now, and they had
their first son. Catherine's young sister, Mary,
only seventeen, often stayed with the family.
But then something terrible happened – one
evening, after a trip to the theatre, Mary
became ill. She died a few hours later, in
Charles's arms. He later wrote in a letter, 'I
have lost the dearest friend . . .' He wore Mary's
ring for the rest of his life. He remembered
her too through a few female characters in his
novels who were 'young, beautiful and good'.
It is no surprise that his next book was not

Mary Hogarth died in Dickens's arms.

all happy. In fact, Dickens wanted to write *Oliver Twist* because he felt strongly
about the country's poor. He wanted to show what life was like for thousands
of people in cities like London. He wanted to write about one of the city's
biggest problems – crime. London was growing fast and there wasn't work for
everybody. More and more people without food or money chose a life of crime.

Dickens also wanted to write about another problem for the country's poor.
When he was a reporter in parliament in 1834, he took notes on the New Poor
Law. Under this law, poor people without jobs could only receive money if they
went to a **workhouse**. These places were like prisons for the poor. Men, women,
boys and girls lived and worked in different parts of the building. They had to
wear special clothes and live in difficult, dirty **condition**s. Like many people,
Dickens hated the New Poor Law and he hated the workhouses. He wrote a
report for a magazine about conditions in a real workhouse. Then he decided to
write a story about a boy who is born in a workhouse.

The story begins when a young woman is found in the street on a cold, wet
night. She has walked a long way and is very tired. She is taken to the local
workhouse, and she has a baby there. As soon as the boy is born, the poor young
mother dies. Mr Bumble, the head of the workhouse, names the boy Oliver
Twist. Oliver was the first child who was a main character in an English novel.

---

workhouse /ˈwɜːkhaʊs/ (n) a place where poor, homeless people lived
condition /kənˈdɪʃən/ (n) the state that something is in

The first part of the book tells us about the young orphan's unhappy life in the workhouse. Dickens wanted his readers to be angry about the terrible conditions for poor children like Oliver Twist. For example, workhouses saved money by giving the people there only small amounts of cheap food. Dickens showed this in one of the most famous scenes in English literature.

The boys in the workhouse are given just one bowl of **gruel** for one of their meals. They know that they must have more food. Somebody must ask for more, and Oliver is chosen. The boy is nine years old.

'Please sir, I want some more.' From *Oliver Twist*

As usual, the boys cleaned their bowls quickly. Then they all began to speak quietly, looking nervously at Oliver.

The boy was afraid, but he was hungry too. Slowly he stood up and walked towards the front of the room. He had his bowl and spoon in his hands. He walked towards the fat man by the big pot of gruel.

The scene in the workhouse is one of the most famous in English literature.

gruel /ˈgruːəl/ (n) a thin food cooked in water. It was eaten by the poor.

'Please, sir, I want some more,' said Oliver.

The fat man with the big spoon could not believe his ears. His two assistants could not believe their ears. Nobody ever asked for more!

The man spoke at last. 'What?!' he said quietly.

'Please, sir,' replied Oliver, 'I want some more.'

This time the man hit Oliver on the head with the spoon and then held the boy's arms. He began to shout for Mr Bumble!

Soon everyone in the workhouse has heard the terrible news – Oliver Twist has asked for more! Oliver is sent away from the workhouse and he begins his adventures. Running off to London, he meets another boy, Jack Dawkins. Jack takes Oliver through the dirty, narrow streets to see an old man with a beard and untidy red hair. The old man, Fagin, seems kind to Oliver at first, but Fagin has

Fagin in the musical film Oliver!

a dark secret. He prepares boys for a life of crime. Every day Jack Dawkins and the others go out on to the streets of London and steal from people. The young thieves bring everything back to Fagin.

Great Dickens Characters: Fagin

Fagin does not seem a bad man at first. When we first see him, he is cooking food for a group of boys. But we learn that Fagin is really only interested in money. He hides a box of rings, gold watches and other expensive things. Every night he takes the box out and looks greedily at these 'pretty things'.

Oliver does not become a criminal, but he has many exciting adventures. He meets the frightening Bill Sikes, a dangerous criminal who steals from people's houses. Bill's girlfriend Nancy is kind to Oliver and tries to help him. The novel has a terrible murder, and it has a mystery too – who is Mr Monks? What does Monks know about Oliver's real family history? Of course, Dickens gives the reader answers to all of these questions and he gives Oliver a happy ending.

The first part of *Oliver Twist* was published in the year Victoria became queen at the age of eighteen. She was still queen when Dickens died. *Oliver Twist* and Dickens's other novels give us an important picture of life in Victorian England – the good and the bad.

Like *Pickwick Papers, Oliver Twist* was very popular. Some people did not like the way that it showed the lives of criminals. In their opinion, the street crime in *Oliver Twist* seemed *too* exciting. But most readers understood Dickens's purpose. And the two biggest criminals – Fagin and Bill Sikes – are both dead by the end of the book. A few readers were not happy about the character of Nancy because she continues to love the terrible Bill Sikes. Dickens wrote defending this character and her love for Sikes.

CHAPTER 4

The Famous Writer

Readers wrote to Dickens, asking him not to 'kill' the character.
All around the country people cried when they read her death scene.

Charles and Catherine had a second child, Mary, before the twenty-fourth, and last, part of *Oliver Twist* was published. His work was more and more popular, but Dickens still worried about money. His parents were a part of his life, and not always a welcome one. John Dickens's money problems continued, and he still asked his famous son for money. He even tried to borrow money from some of Dickens's friends. Finally, Dickens paid for a small house for his parents in the south of England and gave them a little money every year.

Oliver Twist was not finished until November 1839, but Dickens started to publish parts of a new book before that. Again, the title of the novel was the name of the main character – *Nicholas Nickleby*. Again, part of the book came out every month. Readers were happy to receive a new Dickens story, and the first part of *Nicholas Nickleby* sold 50,000 copies.

In *Oliver Twist*, Dickens used the story to give his opinion about conditions in workhouses. In *Nicholas Nickleby*, he attacked bad schools. The subject came straight from the news, and Dickens had strong feelings about it. At the time there were some very bad schools; some of the worst were in Yorkshire, in the north of England. These schools cost money, but the conditions were terrible. Schools sometimes gave their pupils no holidays; the children lived at the school all year. People often sent children there to get them out of the way. The schools were like prisons for children.

Before he began the novel, Dickens visited a few Yorkshire schools with the artist Hablot Knight Browne ('Phiz'). The writer's real name was famous now, and so he used a different name. In one school, Dickens met a **headmaster** called William Shaw. Shaw only had one eye and he was terribly unpleasant to the boys in his school. (He was taken to court because of the terrible conditions in the school.) When Dickens wrote about a headmaster for the school in his book, Shaw was in his mind. Dickens even gave his headmaster, the terrible Wackford Squeers, on eye, just like Shaw.

Great Dickens Characters: Wackford Squeers

The headmaster of Dotheboys Hall is a stupid, unkind man. The boys at the school live in fear of a look from his single, green-grey eye. His wife, son and daughter are as unkind as he is.

headmaster /ˌhedˈmɑːstə/ (n) the teacher in charge of a school

The terrible Wackford Squeers is one of Dickens's best ugly, unkind characters.

In the novel, nineteen-year-old Nicholas Nickleby is sent by his uncle to teach at Squeers' school, Dotheboys Hall. Nickleby cannot believe the terrible conditions at the school. When one poor boy, Smike, tries to run away, Nickleby saves him from Squeers. In a wonderful scene, Nickleby hits the headmaster in front of all the boys in the school. Nickleby leaves the school for London, and Smike soon joins him. The rest of the book follows their adventures. At one point, Smike is caught by Squeers and the poor boy later dies. As in *Oliver Twist*, the ending of the novel gives the reader a surprise secret about the past of one of the characters. We learn that Smike was the son of Nickleby's uncle by a secret marriage.

The book was another success, but most people remember the early chapters in Dotheboys Hall more than the later part of the novel. Dickens's attack on the Yorkshire schools was successful too. Not long after the book was published, headmaster William Shaw's school closed. Most of the similar Yorkshire schools also closed their doors.

A third child was born to Charles and Catherine Dickens after *Nicholas Nickleby*, and the family moved to a nice house in London's Regent's Park. In his next novel, Dickens wrote about another child character – a sweet young girl called Little Nell. At first, he planned a short story in six parts, but in the end it became a novel in forty parts. The book was called *The Old Curiosity Shop*, and Little Nell became Dickens's most popular character at the time. The writer was working harder than ever – this time a new part of the book came out every week.

In the story, young Nell Trent lives with her grandfather He has a small shop, but some terrible characters want the shop. The worst of these is a man called Quilp. He lends money to Nell's grandfather and soon he takes the shop. The girl and the old man have to leave the shop and they travel across the country.

The girl's family find them at last, but they are too late. Nell has become ill and died. It was very difficult for Dickens to write these last scenes in the novel. 'I am slowly murdering that poor child,' he wrote in a letter to a friend. It is clear why the sad death of Little Nell was so hard for Dickens, the writer. He was thinking about the death of his wife's sister, Mary Hogarth.

The death of Little Nell proved how popular Dickens's novels were. Readers wrote to Dickens, asking him not to 'kill' the character. All around the country people cried when they read her death scene. In New York, Dickens's American

Dickens gave full notes to the artist for the picture of Little Nell's death scene. He asked for 'a happy look, if death can'.

readers waited for the ship that carried the last part of the novel. Some could not wait. 'Is Little Nell dead?' they shouted across the water to the ship.

Heart of Stone
For many people at the time, *The Old Curiosity Shop* was Dickens's best book. But for some readers, it is one of the worst. In their opinion, it tries too hard to make the reader sad. Not everyone cried. In the words of the writer Oscar Wilde, a person 'must have a heart of stone to read the death of Little Nell without laughing'!

When *The Old Curiosity Shop* was finished, Dickens returned to another novel – *Barnaby Rudge*. It was Dickens's first story about life in the past – in London, in 1780. At this time crowds of people burned Catholic churches and the homes of Catholic families in London, and freed prisoners. People were angry at first because a new law made the lives of Britain's Catholics easier. But as law and order disappeared, this reason became less important. For a few days the city was very dangerous and people lived in fear.

The crowd scenes are the best in the book. Dickens describes the large groups of angry people well, showing the real dangers to the city. But the book is not usually a favourite with readers. Again, Dickens writes about one of his favourite subjects when the title character is put in a London prison.

Like *The Old Curiosity Shop*, there was a new part of *Barnaby Rudge* every week. It is not surprising that Dickens became more and more tired. He became ill and had to go to hospital. One part of the novel was not published for three weeks.

While he was writing *Barnaby Rudge*, Dickens, still only twenty-nine, made a summer trip to Scotland. In Edinburgh, hundreds and hundreds of people wanted to see the great writer. After he finished the book, Dickens began to make new plans. But these were not for his next novel.

3.1 Were you right?

Look back at your answers to Activity 2.4. Then match the people and the thoughts. Write the numbers.

1 'I can't believe he said that!'   3 'I'm so hungry – and very frightened.'
2 'I'll call him Oliver Twist.'   4 'I'll make him into a thief.'

3.2 What more did you learn?

Match the names on the right with the descriptions of characters in Dickens's novels.

1 This orphan almost becomes a criminal.

2 This terrible teacher has just one eye.

3 He prepares boys for a life of street crime.

4 This young girl's grandfather loses his shop.

5 He becomes a teacher at the age of 19.

6 She is kind and tries to help young Oliver.

Nicholas Nickleby

Nancy

Little Nell

Oliver Twist

Fagin

Wackford Squeers

3.3 Language in use

Look at the sentence on the right. Then write questions or answers below.

> Workhouses saved money **by giving** the people there only small amounts of cheap food.

1 How did Dickens remember Catherine's sister Mary?

..........By wearing her ring..........

2 ....

By making money from crime.

3 How did Dickens show his feelings about workhouses?

....

4 How does Mr Bumble punish Oliver Twist?

....

5 ....

By using boys as thieves.

6 How did Dickens find out about bad schools?

....

3.4 What's next?

In 1842 Dickens went to the United States, a new, young country. Look at the pictures in Chapter 5. What do you think?

1 Who did he go with?

....

2 How did they travel there?

....

3 Did Americans like his writing before he went?

....

4 What did Dickens like about the United States?

....

5 What did he dislike?

....

At Home and Abroad

The American newspapers were less happy
when Dickens gave his opinions of their own country.

Charles and Catherine went to the United States on a ship called the Britannia.

Many Victorian families had a lot of children, and this was true of Charles and Catherine Dickens. But Dickens was an unusual father to his children. Often he was a lot of fun. He enjoyed games and parties. There were many visitors to the house, with much music and laughing.

But there was another side to Dickens the father. Every day, he checked his children's hands and clothes. He went into their rooms and looked through their cupboards carefully. When the rooms were not tidy, Dickens wrote angry notes to his children.

In fact, Dickens's new idea brought a big change to his children's lives. He decided to have a rest from writing and go on a tour of the United States. His novels were very popular there and he had great hopes for the young country. But Dickens did not want to travel alone. He wanted Catherine to go with him.

The two had four children now. Catherine felt ill at the thought of leaving them. But Dickens did not accept her worries. In January 1842 he and Catherine left for the United States. They left their children in London and did not see them for six months. During this time, Catherine's sister Georgina saw the children a lot and became close to them.

Dickens and his wife arrived in Boston to a wonderful welcome. There were crowds in the street waiting to see the famous writer. More people came from all over the country. The American newspapers loved the writer's strong opinions about conditions in England. At first, Dickens liked the US very much. He thought that Boston was a nice, clean city. He visited schools and factories and preferred the conditions in them to schools and factories at home in England.

But as Dickens travelled around the country, he began to like it less and less. He visited a prison and found the conditions very bad. He hated the fact that there were still **slave**s in the US. He was also not happy about how his work was published there. Like other foreign writers, he often received no money for his novels. The American newspapers were less happy when Dickens gave his opinions of their own country. When he returned to England, Dickens quickly wrote a book about his tour, *American Notes*. Some American readers were angry about that book too.

The United States was in his next novel. Again, the title was the name of its main character, but for some time Dickens was unable to choose a name. He thought about the names Chubblewig, Sweezlewag and a few others. At last he chose the name and the book's title – *Martin Chuzzlewit*.

More and more, Dickens thought that each of his novels had one main subject. In *Martin Chuzzlewit* he wanted to write about selfishness. It tells the story of the title character's greedy relatives. Dickens was very happy with the book – his last under the name 'Boz' – but it was not as popular as some of his others.

One newspaper published this unkind picture of Dickens.

slave /sleɪv/ (n) someone who is owned by another person. A *slave* must work without pay.

Perhaps because of this, Dickens added something new to the novel in the sixth part. Martin Chuzzlewit's grandson travels to the US. But the parts of the novel in the US were not popular in that country. Some readers there thought that Dickens was attacking their country again. It is true that most of the American characters seem very interested in money.

The book does have some excellent characters. Perhaps the most famous of these is Mrs Sairey Gamp.

Great Dickens Characters: Mrs Gamp

Mrs Sairey Gamp is a nurse. She is there when babies are born. She is there when people die. Dickens describes her as a fat old woman. Her face and nose are round and red, and she enjoys a drink. Mrs Gamp often speaks to her friend Mrs Harris. There is just one problem – Mrs Harris isn't there!

Mrs Gamp from Martin Chuzzlewit

Another great character from the novel is Seth Pecksniff. In the eyes of others, he seems to be a good man, but he is trying to get his hands on old Martin Chuzzlewit's money too.

After *Martin Chuzzlewit* and Dickens's next story (see Chapter 6), Catherine had another child – their fifth. In a letter, Dickens joked that, after four other children, he did not want to look at the baby. Perhaps there was some true feeling in Dickens's bad joke. He was a rich man, but he always worried about money. Now he had to feed another child.

He decided to move the family to Italy for a year. He thought that life there was cheaper. Also, he planned to write another travel book, because *American Notes* was a success in England.

The family moved to Genoa (Genova) in the summer of 1844. For the next few years Dickens was abroad more than he was at home. The Dickens family went with Catherine's sister, Georgina Hogarth; she was now very close to the family. After writing another long story, Dickens travelled around Italy. He later used his notes for a travel book called *Pictures from Italy*.

Dickens had one very unusual meeting in Italy. In Genoa, he met an English woman called Augusta de la Rue. She was quite ill but, in Dickens's opinion, the problem was in her mind. With his usual interest in modern ideas, Dickens decided to help her. He decided that the answer lay in her early life. (This idea can be seen in his stories, too.) After some time with Dickens, de la Rue's condition became better. But Catherine Dickens was not happy about her husband's time with his 'patient'. Dickens was angry that Catherine felt this way. It was the first problem of many in their marriage.

The family returned to England in the summer of 1845. For a short time Dickens edited a newspaper, but he did not enjoy the work. He was also busy with other ideas; he wanted to be in a play with some friends. This was not surprising. Dickens always loved the theatre. At the end of his North American tour, both he and Catherine acted on the stage in a play.

Catherine continued to have babies. The sixth arrived late in 1845, the next in the spring of 1847. By 1850, Charles and Catherine Dickens had ten children. But this big family was not a sign of a happy marriage. Dickens still had feelings for his wife, but he was not always interested in her now. He preferred to spend time with Catherine's sister, Georgina; she still lived with the family. He did not love her, but he called her his 'best and truest friend'.

Dickens was famous for his descriptions of English life, but he was still not ready to live back in England for very long. In 1846 he moved his family to Switzerland for a few months. He began a new book here, but he did not really enjoy life away from cities. The family moved to Paris for the winter. They only returned to live in England in the spring of 1847.

CHAPTER 6

Dickens and Christmas

For Dickens, Christmas was a time to be kind to other people.
It was also a wonderful time of food and drink, parties and happy families.

Dickens's interest in better conditions for the poor was as strong as ever. He wanted parliament to do more. He wrote a letter to a newspaper calling for new laws about work conditions for women and children. He strongly believed in the need for schools for everybody.

But he also believed that it was not only the government's job to help the poor. In his opinion, people should give more of their own money to help poor people too. This is made clear in one of his most famous stories. In fact, *A Christmas Carol* is one of the most famous stories in the world and Ebenezer Scrooge is probably one of the most famous characters in English literature.

Great Dickens Characters: Ebenezer Scrooge
When we first meet the old man Scrooge, on the day before Christmas, he is mean and unkind. He is a business man with no time for friends or relatives. He loves one thing – money.

A kind family man, Bob Cratchit, works for Scrooge. As usual, Cratchit asks for Christmas Day off work. Scrooge agrees, but he is not happy about this. He hates everything about Christmas. When two men ask him for money for the poor, Scrooge gives them nothing. 'Are there no prisons? Are there no workhouses?' he asks coldly.

Scrooge lives alone, and that night he returns to his empty home. But a terrible surprise is waiting for him. As he stands at his front door, it seems to change before his eyes. Suddenly he is looking into the face of his old **partner**, Jacob Marley. But Marley died seven years ago.

When the face has disappeared, Scrooge runs inside. He looks all around, and nobody is in the house. But then he hears a noise. It gets louder. Something is coming up the stairs . . .

'It is a terrible chain!' From *A Christmas Carol*
'I will not believe it!' said Scrooge to himself.
    But then something came straight through the door and into the room. It was the **ghost** of Jacob Marley! He had the same face, the same clothes. But

partner /ˈpɑːtnə/ (n) a person who you own a business with
ghost /ɡəʊst/ (n) a walking, talking dead person who people can see

now Marley's ghost was pulling a long **chain**. It was made of money boxes and locks and keys and business books.

Scrooge looked into his old partner's dead eyes, and still he did not believe it.
'What do you want?' cried Scrooge.

'A lot!' answered the ghost. The voice was Marley's.

'Who are you?'

'Ask me who I was,' said the ghost.

Scrooge spoke louder. 'Who were you, then?'

'In life, I was your partner, Jacob Marley!'

'This is silly!' cried Scrooge. 'I don't believe it. I am probably seeing you because I ate a bad piece of cheese for dinner!'

In answer, the ghost gave a terrible cry and shook the chains loudly. Scrooge fell to his knees in fear.

'Do you believe in me or not?' said Marley's ghost.

'I do!' cried Scrooge. 'I must. But why are you here? Why are you pulling that chain?'

'I made this chain in my life,' replied the ghost. 'Your own chain was as heavy and long as this seven years ago, Scrooge. And you have worked on it a lot since that time. It is a terrible chain!'

Finally, Scrooge believes that Marley has returned.

chain /tʃeɪn/ (n) a line of metal rings joined together

Marley's ghost tells Scrooge that three more ghosts will visit him that night. The first is the ghost of Christmas Past. This ghost shows Scrooge scenes from his own past. We see that Ebenezer was not always unkind. In fact, he was a lonely boy. (It is interesting that Ebenezer's sister is called Fan. Dickens's own older sister was called Fanny. Did Dickens see part of his own character in the young Scrooge?)

This part of the novel shows one of Dickens's strong opinions – the character of an adult is shaped by his or her life as a child. The reader is shown more scenes of Scrooge's early life. He grows up and joins the world of business. We watch as his heart becomes colder and colder.

When Scrooge sees the second ghost, it is sitting happily on a great pile of Christmas food. This ghost takes Scrooge and shows him scenes of Christmas now. People cannot see Scrooge, but he can see them. They visit Scrooge's only relative, and they visit the family of his office worker, Bob Cratchit. The Cratchit family have no money and one of their children, Tiny Tim, is not well. But their Christmas is happy and full of love.

The second ghost

Before the second ghost leaves, he shows Scrooge two children, a boy and a girl. The boy is Stupidity and the girl is Want. The ghost tells Scrooge that both are dangerous. But the boy is the most dangerous of all. For Dickens, this scene is the heart of the story.

The third and final ghost frightens Scrooge the most. This is the ghost of Christmas in the future. Scrooge learns about Bob Cratchit's son, Tiny Tim. Without medicine or good food, the boy will die. The ghost also shows Scrooge the world after he has died. In this future, nobody is interested in the lonely death of a mean old man.

Scrooge wakes in fear. Then he learns that it is Christmas morning. Only one night has passed. Scrooge's heart jumps with happiness. He realises that he can change his life. It is not too late. He understands at last

Scrooge is a different man when he wakes up on Christmas morning.

that money is not everything. It is more important to be kind. After this, he is
happy and kind to other people. He visits his relatives. He gives Bob Cratchit
more money, and he is 'a second father' to Bob's ill son, Tiny Tim.

A Christmas Carol is a simple story, and the novel is not very long. Dickens
wrote it in just six weeks. The book was published in December 1843, and
readers loved it. In a way, Dickens's story helped to change the idea of Christmas
in England. Before that time, Christmas was probably a less important time
for Christians than Easter. For Dickens, Christmas was a time to be kind to
other people. It was also a wonderful time of food and drink, parties and happy
families.

The story is still popular today all around the world. There have been a lot of
films of it – there is even a Disney film of the story with Mickey Mouse as Bob
Cratchit! Why is this story so popular? Perhaps because it asks the reader serious
questions. What is really important in life? What makes a life good or happy?

After the great success of *A Christmas Carol*, Dickens decided to write a
Christmas story every year. He wrote five, but none of the other books had the
same success as the story of Scrooge.

4.1 Were you right?

1 **Look back at your answers to Activity 3.4. Then finish the newspaper report about Dickens's trip in 1842.**

In 1842 Dickens travelled to .... His .... went with him, but his .... stayed at home in London. In Boston big .... waited to see the writer. At first, Dickens .... the United States very much. But he did not like slavery or the conditions in American .... When Dickens spoke about money for foreign writers in the US, some American .... attacked him.

4.2 What more did you learn?

1 **Are these sentences right (✓) or wrong (✗)?**

a ☐ Martin Chuzzlewit was very popular in the United States.

b ☐ Mrs Gamp is a character in Martin Chuzzlewit.

c ☐ Catherine and Charles Dickens were very happy together in Italy.

d ☐ Catherine's sister Georgina started living with the family.

e ☐ In *A Christmas Carol*, Scrooge's old partner is called Bob Cratchit.

f ☐ Scrooge is shown the scene of his own death.

g ☐ Dickens wrote more Christmas stories after *A Christmas Carol*.

2 **Finish these sentences.**

a Ebenezer Scrooge is a character in ....

b At the beginning of the story, Scrooge is only interested in money. At the end of the story, he understands that ....

c For years, Scrooge has had no time for family. At the end of the story, he starts ....

d Scrooge has not paid Bob Cratchit much money. At the end of the story, he ....

e At the beginning, Scrooge thinks that the poor should be in prison. At the end of the story, he believes that people should ....

.3 Language in use

Look at the sentence on the right. Then rewrite the sentences below.

> Some American readers there **thought that** Dickens **was attacking** their country again.

1 What did Dickens think?

Dickens thought that Boston was a nice, clean city

> Boston is a nice, clean city.

2 What did he believe?

> The use of slaves is wrong.

3 What did he learn?

> Americans don't like attacks on their country.

4 What did he think?

> Everybody should go to school.

5 What did he believe?

> I can teach people through my stories.

.4 What's next?

There is a lot in Dickens's stories about his own life. Which real people do you think gave him ideas for these characters?

| strongly believes in her husband | dies young and beautiful | spends time in a debtors' prison | works in a London factory |

1 .... **2** .... **3** .... **4** ....

CHAPTER 7

The Writer's Life

This novel was the closest to Dickens's own life.
It is told by the character of David Copperfield.

Dickens's next novel, *Dombey and Son*, was about a proud business man. The rich character Paul Dombey thinks that his son will continue the family name. He does not have time for his loving daughter Florence. By the end of the book, Dombey has learned a hard lesson about life and family.

Dombey and Son was published in twenty monthly parts. But for the first time Dickens wrote notes, carefully planning the story. Again, the city of London is like a character in the novel. Dickens wrote about the city like no other writer, with both love and hate. At about this time, the city's new railway stations were built. Dickens understood how important these stations were. In *Dombey and Son*, the railway is a sign of the new face of the city.

While he was abroad, Dickens was not just thinking about his next book. He was thinking about his own past, and he began to write about it. Back in England, he told a friend, John Forster, about his time at the boot polish factory. He and Forster talked more about Dickens's past. Dickens's older sister Fanny died in 1848, and perhaps this also brought more painful memories of the past. He continued to write about his own life.

He showed these notes to Catherine. In her opinion, they were too honest in their description of Dickens's parents. She thought that he should not publish family secrets like this. Dickens listened to Catherine this time, but he did not throw the work away. He put much of it into his next novel, *David Copperfield*. Again, the title was the name of the main character. This story was the closest to Dickens's own life and it is told by the character of David Copperfield.

David is born in the country. Like Dickens, he is born on a Friday. Some people say this is unlucky. David's father has been dead for six months. His father's aunt, Miss Betsey Trotwood, arrives for the birth. She is surprised that the baby is not a girl. She hits the doctor and leaves the house!

Later, David's mother marries a second husband. This man, Edward Murdstone, does not like David and he is very unkind to him. He sends David away to a terrible school. Here the boy has to wear a sign around his neck: 'He bites.' The school's headmaster, Creakle, joins Wackford Squeers in Dickens's list of terrible teachers.

But soon conditions get worse for David. His mother dies when he is nine. Then Murdstone sends him to work in a bottle factory in London. Of course,

Dickens was remembering his own time at the boot polish factory. In London, David lives with the Micawbers. This family never have enough money.

Great Dickens Characters:
Mr and Mrs Micawber

Dickens writes that there is no more hair on Mr Wilkins Micawber's head than on an egg! Micawber tries to dress well, but his clothes are old. He enjoys the sound of his own voice. He always spends more money than he has. He lives in hope that something good will happen. But he cannot keep a job and at one point in the story is sent to a debtors' prison. Of course, the character of Mr Micawber is very similar to Dickens's father, John Dickens.

Micawber's wife, Emma, is a thin woman who is always feeding a baby. She strongly believes in her husband. She suffers from the family's continuing money problems, but will never leave him. There is very possibly something of Dickens's mother in Mrs Micawber too.

Mr Micawber is one of Dickens's most famous characters.

Dickens poured all his own unhappy memories into this part of the book. But life is even worse for David Copperfield than for the young Charles Dickens. Nobody takes Copperfield away from the bottle factory, so he decides to run away. And so he begins his long, hard walk to Dover, on the south coast of England. This is where his father's aunt, Miss Betsey Trotwood, lives. On the way, David is robbed. When he arrives in Dover, he has nothing. He is tired, hungry and thirsty.

'I am David Copperfield.' From *David Copperfield*

I went into a little shop and asked about Miss Trotwood. A young woman in the shop turned around quickly.

'I work for Miss Trotwood,' she said. 'What do you want with her?'

'I want to speak to her,' I replied.

The woman looked me up and down. 'You want to ask her for money,' she said.

'No!' But her words were true. I had nothing. I was here to ask my father's aunt for money. My face became red.

I followed the young woman to a little house. The front garden was full of flowers.

'This is Miss Trotwood's house,' said the woman. Then she went inside, leaving me at the garden gate. My legs were shaking. I looked terrible. My shoes had holes in them, and my clothes were dirty.

Suddenly I saw a face at the window. It was an old man with grey hair. He was laughing at me. Then the door opened and Miss Betsey Trotwood came out. She was wearing gardening clothes and she had a knife in one hand.

'Go away!' she shouted without looking at me. 'No boys here!'

But I did not leave. 'Please,' I began.

Miss Trotwood looked up.

'Please, aunt,' I said.

She was very surprised. 'What?'

'Please,' I continued. 'I am David Copperfield.'

Miss Trotwood opened her mouth in surprise and sat down on the garden path.

Miss Trotwood is surprised by David Copperfield's visit.

We learn that the man at the window is called Mr Dick. He lives in Miss Trotwood's house. Both of them are kind to David. When Mr Murdstone and his unpleasant sister try to take David, Miss Trotwood sends them away.

The novel is full of wonderful characters. Some of them are kind and good and some, like Murdstone and the terrible office worker Uriah Heep, are very, very bad. David marries Dora Spenlow, but she dies. Then he finally realises that he has always loved another woman, Agnes. The two are happily married.

Of course, *David Copperfield* is a story, but a lot of it is similar to Dickens's own life:

- Their names have the same first letters – DC and CD. (Dickens was very surprised when a friend told him this.)
- The character moves from the country to London.
- The characters of Mr and Mrs Micawber are similar to Dickens's parents.
- David Copperfield has to work in a factory in London. He is as unhappy there as Dickens was in the polish factory.
- David's love for Dora Spenlow is like Dickens's love for Maria Beadnell. Dickens's description of Dora is very similar to Maria.
- When he wrote Dora's death scene, perhaps he was thinking again about the death of Mary Hogarth.
- The adult David Copperfield becomes a writer.

Perhaps because it was so close to his own life, Dickens later called *David Copperfield* his 'favourite son'. Many readers agreed with him and *David Copperfield* is still one of the most popular of Dickens's novels.

CHAPTER 8

Defender of the Poor

When they think of London, many people still think of fog. The famous first lines of
Bleak House *helped to give this picture of London to the world.*

Dickens continued to work hard. He never stopped writing for magazines and newspapers. In 1850 he started editing a new magazine. He also wrote hundreds of reports and stories for this magazine. In some of them he gave his opinions about conditions in the country. Other pieces of writing were more personal. Once, he took a quick break from *David Copperfield* and wrote 'A Child's Dream of a Star'. He later wrote about how wonderful this was. Dickens knew that he was not like other people.

The new magazine had fiction and other pieces of writing. It started with around 100,000 readers, and it stayed popular for years. But the times were not all happy for Dickens. Sadly, *David Copperfield* was a mirror of Dickens's real life in another way. The character Dora dies in the book, and now Dickens's baby daughter of the same name died. More sad news came quickly: at about the same time, his father John Dickens died. After all the years of money problems, Dickens forgave his 'poor father' everything.

Dickens did not want to stay in the house where his little Dora died. The family moved again, to another part of London. While some work on the house was finished, they stayed on the coast. In these unhappy conditions, Dickens began his next novel, *Bleak House*.

When they think of London, many people still think of **fog**. The famous first lines of *Bleak House* helped to give this picture of London to the world. The book begins with just two words: 'Fog everywhere.' Dickens continues with a description of thick fog along the River Thames. But Dickens was not only describing the city and its weather. In *Bleak House*, he wrote angrily about the city's law courts. In his opinion, it was easy to get lost in these. Like a fog, people could not find their way through them. Again, Dickens wrote about lawyers. Again, he was not kind about people who worked in the law. At the start of the novel, a court case about Bleak House has continued for a long time. By the end of the case, all the money has gone to the lawyers.

Bleak House has many characters, showing all sides of London life, rich and poor. In some ways, it is a very modern novel. For the first time, Dickens wrote part of the book in the voice of a female character – 18-year-old Esther Summerson. The story is also partly a detective story. The character of Bucket is the first police detective in English fiction.

fog /fɒg/ (n) cloudy air near the ground

Jo has a hard life on the streets of London.

Great Dickens Characters: Jo

With the sad character of Jo, Dickens again showed his strong feelings about the lives of poor street children in the city. The boy clears a path on dirty, busy streets before somebody crosses. This is his only way of earning a little money. He has not been to school and he does not know about his own family or past. He does not know that people have more than one name. He does not know that the name 'Jo' is short for a longer name, Joseph. He cannot even spell the name. Of all of Dickens's characters, lonely Jo is one of the saddest.

Bleak House was a great success for Dickens. It sold more copies than his early books, and Dickens stopped worrying about money for a few months. After more travels in Europe with friends, he began another story for his magazine. In this next novel, *Hard Times*, Dickens faced the new changes in the country's working conditions. In 1838, when he was a reporter, he visited the **mills** in the north of the country. Now, in 1853, he went back to Manchester to prepare for the book. He worried about the lives of working people in this hard, new world of factories and mills. Workers were almost like machines.

Hard Times was a difficult book for Dickens to write. A new part was published every week. Dickens wrote for six months and became more and more tired. The novel is less funny than many of his other stories. In the story

mill /mɪl/ (n) a factory that makes cloth

Conditions were hard in many Victorian workplaces.

of Stephen Blackpool, Dickens attacked the rich owners of mills and factories. In Dickens's opinion, in their search for money these people sometimes forgot about their workers. The message of the book was clear. Dickens wanted to defend poor workers from bad conditions. He wanted factory owners to think about more than just money.

Many of Dickens's most famous stories happen in real places – often London. But for *Hard Times* he thought of a fictional town – Coketown. This was a terrible place of factories and mills. Its red buildings were black from smoke. Its river was dark and dirty. Machines shook the town's windows all day long.

The book also introduces subjects that were more personal for Dickens. The writer was less and less happy with his marriage to Catherine. The book's main character Steven Blackpool does not love his wife. His marriage has failed, but he cannot be with his true love, Rachael.

Hard Times was a success. But some people thought that Dickens's answers to the big problems of the day were too simple. In fact, at about this time some people asked Dickens to become a politician. He refused. He preferred to change things and defend the poor through his written works.

He also tried to help in more practical ways. A good friend of his was a very rich woman called Angela Burdett-Coutts. Coutts wanted to help people with her money, and for years Dickens helped her to do that. For example, Coutts started a home for young women without homes or money. Dickens chose the house and the people who lived there.

Dickens was as popular and busy as ever, but he was not happy. He did not really enjoy time with his wife Catherine; he was tired of her. He was not always happy with his children. He was closer to his daughters, but he wanted his sons to be more like him. He was sad and angry when they were not. Charley, his oldest son, did not know what to do with his life at the age of seventeen.

This was hard for a man like Dickens to understand. For him, there was only one answer to any problem – work and more work. This was just a part of his character.

Dickens with two of his daughters

5.1 Were you right?

Look back at your answers to Activity 4.4. Then complete this information.

> When Dickens wrote about .... , he was probably thinking of
> his father. His father spent time in a .... prison when Dickens
> was a child. But Dickens's mother always believed in her husband, just like
> .... The description of young .... working in a
> dirty factory comes from Dickens's early life. Dickens worked in a
> .... factory. As a young man, Dickens was very close to
> .... He was very sad when she died. Perhaps he was thinking
> of her when he wrote the death scene of ....

5.2 What more did you learn?

Write the correct book title next to the sentences.

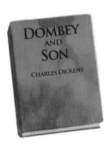
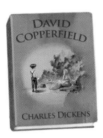

1   The main character walks to his aunt's house.   ....

2   Factory owners in the town of Coketown
    do not look after their workers.   ....

3   A poor street child does not know
    his own last name.   ....

4   A rich man has no time for his loving
    daughter, Florence.   ....

5   Law courts are compared to a thick fog.   ....

6   The main character's young wife dies.   ....

5.3 Language in use

Look at the sentences on the right. Then put the right noun into the second sentence below so it has a similar meaning to the first.

> Dickens continues with a **description** of thick fog along the River Thames. But Dickens was not only **describing** the city and its weather.

1 Miss Betsey is there when David is born.

Miss Betsey is there at David's ....

2 Dickens remembered his own time at the factory.

Dickens used his own .... of factory work.

3 David marries Dora, but she dies.

Dora dies after her .... to David.

4 After she dies, he marries Agnes.

After her .... , he marries Agnes.

5 Dickens edited a magazine.

Dickens was the .... of a magazine.

6 Dickens felt strongly about children like Jo.

Dickens had strong .... about children like Jo.

5.4 What's next?

Read the first few lines of Chapter 9 quickly. What do you think was 'calling to him' from the past? What was Dickens remembering when:

1 he bought the house at Gad's Hill Place?

....

2 he went to see Maria Beadnell?

....

3 he wrote about a man in debtors' prison?

....

4 he fell in love with an 18-year-old woman?

....

Voices from the Past

Again and again in his work, he visited people and places from his memory.
Now the past was calling to him in his life too.

Gad's Hill Place

While Dickens worked, he usually went for long walks. These walks often took him near places from his past. In fact, for Dickens, the past was never far away. Again and again in his stories, he visited people and places from his memory. Now the past was calling to him in his life too.

First, he saw Gad's Hill Place. Remembering his father's words from years before, he decided to buy the house. Soon after this, a letter arrived on his desk. It was another voice from the past – his first love, Maria Beadnell. She did not return his love when he was a young man. But now she was writing to him. In his warm reply, Dickens wrote of the happiness that he remembered with Maria. His letter even spoke about the Maria character in *David Copperfield*, Dora Spenlow. Maria wrote that she was a different woman now. In her own words, she was fat, old and ugly. But memories were too strong for Dickens — he wanted to meet her. To his surprise, Maria's description of herself was true. She still acted in the same way, but now she seemed sad and silly to Dickens. He left the meeting early and did not reply to Maria's letters. (But he did unkindly put a character similar to Maria in a novel again. Flora Finching in *Little Dorrit* is a sad and silly character.)

Dickens began his next novel in these unhappy conditions. It is no surprise that his past plays a large part in the book. In *Bleak House* he attacked the law courts, and in *Hard Times* he attacked work conditions in factories and mills. Now in *Little Dorrit* he chose to attack a different part of English life – prisons. But this subject was more personal for Dickens. When he wrote the story of Amy Dorrit and her father, he was remembering his own father's time in a debtors' prison. The character William Dorrit is in the same prison as Dickens's father – Marshalsea. Of course, the book describes conditions in the prison very clearly because Dickens remembered the place well.

But the character of William Dorrit is very different from David Copperfield's friend, Wilkins Micawber. Micawber was like Dickens's father in many ways, but Dorrit is a much sadder character. This shy, friendly man has been in Marshalsea Prison for twenty-five long years. He calls himself 'the Father of Marshalsea'. Perhaps Dickens's memories of his father were changed by his death. There is not much in the sad character of William Dorrit that readers can find amusing.

Great Dickens Characters: Amy Dorrit

William Dorrit's daughter Amy – the Little Dorrit of the book's title – pays the greatest price for her father's debt. She was born in Marshalsea Prison and lives there with the rest of the Dorrit family. At the age of thirteen, Amy knows that her father is a broken man. She knows, too, that he cannot be a good father to his children. Amy is the oldest of the three Dorrit children, and she is the head of the family. Dickens describes Amy's life as a 'different prison'.

Amy has lived all her life in Marshalsea Prison.

The success of *Little Dorrit* paid for Gad's Hill Place in 1856. Dickens returned to his interest in the theatre, working on a play for the theatre with his friend, the writer Wilkie Collins. Dickens acted in the play, and Georgina Hogarth and a few of Dickens's children did too. Dickens loved acting again, and the play was a great success. Queen Victoria even asked Dickens and the other actors to bring the play to Buckingham Palace, but Dickens refused. He did not want the queen to see his children acting except on a professional stage. So the queen came to see the play at the theatre. She wanted to meet Dickens after the play, but he refused again. This time, it was because he was wearing unsuitable stage clothes. Queen Victoria was not angry, and later thanked Dickens for the play in a warm letter.

After the play's first success, Dickens had bigger plans for it. He took it to Manchester and employed professional actresses. One of these was Frances Ternan, and her two daughters, Maria and Ellen, were actresses too. Maria Ternan had the main female part in the play, but Dickens was most interested in Ellen. She became the last great love of his life.

Dickens was forty-five. He was married (unhappily) and he had a large family. Ellen was only eighteen – the same age as Dickens's daughter Kate. This did not matter to Dickens; his love for Ellen was deep. When Catherine learned about Dickens's feelings, her discovery brought their marriage to an end.

It is impossible to know Dickens's true feelings for Ellen. Why did he love this young woman? Was the past calling him again? Ellen was only one year older than Mary Hogarth when she died in Dickens's arms many years before.

Dickens started to say that Catherine was not a good mother. This was not true, but perhaps he believed it. In his opinion, the girls changed when they were with her. Catherine was very angry, and in May, 1858 she moved out of the family home. Their oldest son, Charley, went with her, but the other children stayed with their father. Catherine's sister Georgina also stayed with Dickens. She lived with him until he died.

Catherine lived alone for the rest of her life. Unkindly, Dickens wrote, 'I want to forgive her and forget her.' Years later, their daughter Kate defended their mother and saw more and more of her. When Catherine was dying in 1879 – nine years after her husband's death – she gave Kate all Charles's letters to her. She asked Kate to give them to the nation. Catherine wanted the world to know that he loved her.

CHAPTER 10

Dickens on Stage

*As he looked at himself in the mirror, he was talking, but not with his usual voice.
He was acting – being the characters in his novels.*

The life of a writer is usually quiet, but Charles Dickens was not usual in any way. He could not live a quiet life. We know that he always loved the theatre. He could copy a lot of different voices. When he was young, he wanted to be a professional actor. He acted in a few plays at different times, and he was a great success.

In fact, Dickens's love of the theatre and his work as a writer were not very different. One of his daughters remembered a story about her father. He was writing a book at his desk, but every few minutes he stood up. He walked to a mirror and began to put on the faces of his different characters. As he looked at himself in the mirror, he was talking, but not with his usual voice. He was acting – *being* the characters in his novels.

In fact, for years Dickens often tested stories by reading them to friends. Sometimes he read parts from his books to crowds in theatres. He usually gave the money to the poor. After *Little Dorrit* was published, Dickens decided to do more of these readings. A month before Catherine left the family home, he planned a tour of theatres. One of his close friends did not like the idea, but Dickens did not change his mind. 'I must *do* something,' he wrote. He also understood that this was a good business idea. This time, Dickens planned to keep the money from the tour.

Dickens was still very popular, but the newspapers were full of stories about the end of his marriage. There were a lot of questions. Did he love Ellen Ternan? Did he love Georgina Hogarth? Some of the newspapers attacked him. In his novels, he always wrote warmly about strong, happy families. The message was that nothing was more important in life. But in his *own* life, Dickens was ending his marriage; he did not hide his feelings for a woman the same age as his own daughter. Some of Dickens's friends worried. Perhaps, after all this, Dickens was not so popular with the British people?

There was no need to worry. Dickens began the tour in London. When he first walked on stage, the crowd in the theatre was very excited. The same happened on the rest of the tour. Dickens always started on time, walking on to the stage with a flower in his jacket. He had a book in his hands, but he really did not need it. Dickens could remember the scenes perfectly.

When he began to read, he seemed to change. His voice was different and he even looked different. He seemed to *become* each new character – the clever

Dickens on stage

Sam Weller from *Pickwick Papers*, the nurse Mrs Gamp from *Martin Chuzzlewit*, the mean old man Scrooge from *A Christmas Carol*. The crowds laughed at the funny characters. Hundreds of people cried during the sad scenes. The tour was a great success, leaving Dickens happy but tired. A second national tour in the winter of 1858 was also successful.

After these tours, Dickens planned a new magazine. As usual, he started a book for the magazine. The story – *A Tale of Two Cities* – was Dickens's first historical novel since *Barnaby Rudge*. The two cities of the title were Paris and London, and Dickens was writing about the French **Revolution** of 1789. The first words of the book are very famous: 'It was the best of times, it was the worst of times . . .' Of course, Dickens wanted the novel to have a message for the present day. If most people do not have good schools and good work conditions, it is dangerous for everybody.

A Tale of Two Cities told the history of the Revolution, but it was also a love story, and readers never forget Sydney Carton.

Great Dickens Characters: Sydney Carton

At first the English lawyer is described as selfish and lazy. He looks very similar to Darnay. He loves the same woman, Lucie, but she loves Darnay. At the end of the novel, Darnay is going to be killed in Paris by revolutionaries. For the love

---

revolution /ˌrevəˈluːʃən/ (n) a time when the people of a country change their form of government completely. A *revolutionary* is a person who fights for that change.

of Lucie, Carton takes Darnay's place. Darnay escapes and returns to Lucie. In the book's famous last scene, Carton goes bravely to his death. He is doing 'a far, far better thing . . . than I have ever done.'

A Tale of Two Cities was shorter than most of Dickens's other works, and it was much more serious, but readers loved it. Dickens described it as 'the best story I have ever written'.

Perhaps Dickens was thinking about himself and Ellen Ternan when he wrote Sydney Carton's romantic last scene. But Dickens did not lose Ellen. He saw her often, paying for a house for her and her family in London. In 1859, Ellen stopped acting in the theatre. This was probably Dickens's idea.

In 1860, Dickens decided to make Gad's Hill Place his main home. He kept a flat in London for short visits to the city. At about this time he burned all his personal letters and papers in a great fire. After that, Dickens destroyed every new personal letter. More than ever, the most famous writer in the country wanted a private life.

Many readers have cried at Carton's brave last words.

6.1 Were you right?

Look back at your answers to Activity 5.4. Then answer the questions.

1 Why did Dickens buy the house at Gad's Hill Place?

....

2 What did he think of Maria Beadnell when he met her again?

....

3 How was the story of *Little Dorrit* similar to Dickens's own life?

....

4 In what way was Ellen Ternan like Catherine Dickens's sister, Mary Hogarth?

....

6.2 What more did you learn?

1 Match the names and the thoughts.

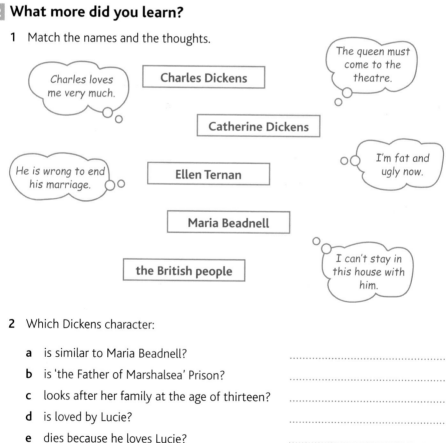

2 Which Dickens character:

    a is similar to Maria Beadnell? ....

    b is 'the Father of Marshalsea' Prison? ....

    c looks after her family at the age of thirteen? ....

    d is loved by Lucie? ....

    e dies because he loves Lucie? ....

6.3 Language in use

**Look at the sentence on the right.
Then put the right forms of the verbs
in the sentences below.**

> When Catherine **was dying** in 1879,
> she **gave** Kate all Charles's letters to her.

1 Dickens ....*was walking*.......... (walk) through the streets when he
   .... (see) the house at Gad's Hill Place.

2 When he was acting in a play, he .... (meet) Ellen Ternan.

3 Perhaps he was thinking about his love for Ellen when he ....
   (write) the novel's last romantic scene.

4 Most of Dickens's children .... (live) with their mother when
   Dickens moved to Gad's Hill Place.

5 When Dickens was writing, he .... (stand up) every few
   minutes.

6.4 What's next?

**Look at the pictures in Chapter 11 from Dickens's next novel, *Great
Expectations*. What do you think? Are these sentences right (✓) or wrong (✗)?**

1 ☐ The boy in the picture on page 49 is the main character in the book.

2 ☐ The man in the same picture is the boy's father.

3 ☐ The boy is afraid when he sees the man.

4 ☐ The woman in the picture on page 50 is the boy's grandmother.

5 ☐ The old woman is very rich.

6 ☐ The old woman loves the boy.

7 ☐ The boy starts to love the girl in the same picture.

CHAPTER 11

Money and Crime

Like David Copperfield, *the new novel returned to Dickens's own past. But Dickens was older now. His view of his past life was less simple.*

Now living at Gad's Hill Place without Catherine, Dickens continued to take long walks every day. These walks took him to many places from his past. All these memories helped to shape his next novel, *Great Expectations.* Before he started, Dickens read *David Copperfield* again. He did not want the two books to be too similar. Like *David Copperfield,* the new novel returned to Dickens's own past. But Dickens was older now. His view of his past life was less simple.

Great Expectations is the story of Philip Pirrip – 'Pip'. Like David Copperfield, the main character in the book tells the story to the reader. As a boy, Pip lives in a village with his older sister because his parents are dead. She is married to a kind, simple man called Joe Gargary. The boy likes Joe very much, but Pip's sister – 'Mrs Joe' – is not a pleasant character.

The novel begins with a famous scene. Pip is outside the local church, in the place where his parents lie. He thinks that he is alone in the fog. But suddenly a terrible voice shouts to him. A large man jumps out. He is wet and dirty and cold. 'Don't move or I will kill you!' shouts the man. The young boy is very frightened, but he cannot escape. This is Pip's first meeting with Abel Magwitch. This meeting changes Pip's life forever.

Great Dickens Characters: Abel Magwitch

The man, Abel Magwitch, has escaped from one of the prison ships off the coast. (At this time, many British prisoners were sent to live in Australia. When Dickens was a boy, he saw the prison ships in the sea near England's south coast.) The prisoner tells Pip to find him some food. He also needs a tool because he wants to cut the chain from his leg. If Pip does not come back, Magwitch will kill him. In fear, Pip brings Magwitch food and helps him to escape from his chains. Magwitch is a frightening character at first. But we learn that he is grateful for Pip's help.

Magwitch is caught, but he does not tell anybody about Pip's help. He is sent to Australia but he never forgets the young boy. Of course, this is not the end of Magwitch's part in *Great Expectations.*

One day, Pip's sister comes home with news. There is a rich old woman in town called Miss Havisham. She has sent an unusual message. She wants Pip to come to her house and to play there. Pip is dressed in his best clothes. Joe's uncle, Pumblechook, takes the nervous boy to Miss Havisham's house. The house is big and dark with bars on many of the windows. Pip and Pumblechook wait at the front gate. An older girl with keys in her hand comes to open the gate. Nervously, Pip goes with her, leaving Pumblechook outside at the gate.

Pip's meeting with Magwitch is one of Dickens's most famous first chapters.

'I want to go home.' From *Great Expectations*

I followed the girl into the house and up the dark stairs. She pointed to a door.

'Go in,' she said.

The room was large. There were lights all around, but there was no light from outside. A strange old woman was sitting at a table with a mirror. She was wearing white shoes and a white dress – a wedding dress. There were flowers in her white hair. There seemed to be no life in her eyes.

The old lady turned her pale face. 'Who is it?' she said.

'Pip,' I replied. 'I have come to play.'

I noticed that the hands of the clock did not move. The time in this room was always twenty to nine. The old lady's watch showed the same time.

'Look at me,' said Miss Havisham. 'I have not seen the sun since you were born. Are you afraid of me?'

'No,' I said, but this was not true.

Miss Havisham put her hand on her chest and asked, 'Do you know what I touch here?'

Pip does not know why he was invited to Miss Havisham's house.

'Your heart.'

'It is broken!' said the old woman with a strange smile. Then she said, 'I am tired. Call Estella and play.'

The girl came to the room and we decided to play a game of cards.

'What can you play, boy?' she asked me coldly. I told her and we began the game. She won easily.

Suddenly Estella said, 'Look at his hands! And his thick boots! He is just a stupid village boy!'

Miss Havisham smiled. 'What do you think of her?' she asked me.

'I think that she is proud,' I said quietly.

'And?'

'I think that she is very pretty.'

'And?'

'I think that she is rude,' I said.

'And?'

'And I think that I want to go home.'

Miss Havisham hates all men. She enjoys it when Estella is unkind to Pip. But even after this meeting, Pip begins to love Estella. The rest of the book follows Pip as he becomes a man. We learn that a mysterious person has given him a lot of money. For years, Pip believes that this comes from Miss Havisham. For much of the book, Pip is selfish. He thinks that money makes him better than other people. But then Abel Magwitch returns with surprising news. The money was *not* Miss Havisham's. Magwitch earned a lot of money in Australia. Remembering the kind boy outside the church, he sent the money to Pip. All Pip's money came from a criminal! When he learns this, Pip has to change his opinion of the world and his own place in it. There are some very famous scenes near the end of the novel. A fire destroys Miss Havisham's house, and Pip and Magwitch try to escape from the London police on the River Thames.

At first, Dickens did not want the book to have a happy ending. In his first ending, Pip finally learns that Estella will never return his love. But a friend changed Dickens's mind about this and he wrote a different ending. The novel was published with this new ending. Pip returns to England after eleven years abroad. He revisits Miss Havisham's house, lost in memories. Estella is there, too. She has been married, but her husband is dead. She asks Pip to be kind and leave her alone. But in his heart Pip knows that the two will stay together now.

Pip and Estella are given a happy ending, but this was not true for the novel's writer. Dickens wanted to live with Ellen Ternan, but this was not possible with Catherine alive.

CHAPTER 12

Last Years

*There are a lot of questions in the first part of the novel,
but we have no answers to the mystery. Dickens never finished the book.*

Dickens began his last full novel, *Our Mutual Friend*, in 1864. The work was not easy. It took him longer to write each new part now. Dickens was becoming more and more unwell, but he still went for a long walk every day. In June, 1865 he travelled to France with Ellen and her mother. On the way back to London from the coast, the train crashed. Ten passengers died. Dickens and the Ternans were not hurt, but their part of the train hung from a bridge over a river. Dickens helped Ellen and her mother off the train. Then he began to help the other passengers. He stayed with the people who were hurt and dying. He used his hat to carry water from the river. After a few hours, he remembered that that month's part of *Our Mutual Friend* was still on the train. The conditions were very dangerous, but Dickens went back and found his work.

In *Our Mutual Friend*, Dickens seems to attack London, calling it a 'hopeless city' with its 'great black river'. The book begins on this river, as Jess Hexham and his daughter Lizzie search the Thames for dead bodies. They earn money by finding bodies in the water. In fact, many of the characters in

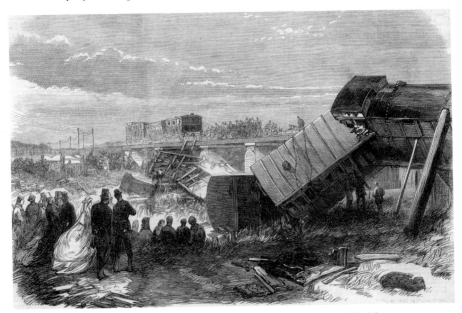

After this crash, Dickens was a nervous traveller for the rest of his life.

Our Mutual Friend are shaped by their need for money. Dickens paints a dark picture of the world in his last full novel. He was still very angry about the country's workhouses and prisons. Until the end of his life, Dickens was still fighting to make things better.

After the book was published, Dickens was invited back to the United States. Remembering his first visit there, he was not sure about this idea. But finally, he agreed. He wanted Ellen to join him there, but she was ill. He missed her during the tour, but it was still a great success. Some Americans remembered him from his tour in 1842, twenty-five years earlier. They were surprised at the changes in the writer. Now he looked old and ill. But the problem was not just the writer's health. Dickens was less and less happy.

Back in England, he started his last tour reading from his books. Wanting this tour to be the best of all, he chose a famous scene from *Oliver Twist*. At first he told friends, 'I am afraid to try it.' But soon he was reading the scene in theatres. In it, the terrible criminal Bill Sikes kills Nancy, because she wants to help Oliver. Dickens acted the scene with great feeling and the crowds listened in surprised silence. But Dickens was feeling ill all the time. He was in pain and he could not see well. Soon he could not say the names of some of his characters on stage. He stopped the tour before the end.

In August, 1869 he began one more novel. *The Mystery of Edwin Drood* was another dark story. The character of the title, Edwin Drood, disappears one Christmas after a storm. Is he dead? Was he murdered by his uncle, John Jasper? There are a lot of questions in the first part of the novel, but we have no answers to the mystery. Dickens never finished the book.

While he was working on *The Mystery of Edwin Drood*, Dickens read from his books in a London theatre for the last time. He chose *A Christmas Carol*, one of the crowd's favourites. He cried as he said goodbye to the crowd. He also met Queen Victoria at last, when she invited him to Buckingham Palace.

In June, 1870, his favourite child, Kate, visited him at Gad's Hill Place. She told him about her plans to be an actress. Dickens asked her to choose a different profession. He spoke to her for a long time, telling her many things about his past. He was sorry that he was not a better father, a better man.

A few days later, Dickens was eating dinner with Georgina after a full day's work when he became ill. He jumped up from the table, wanting to go to London. Then he fell to the floor. The children were called to see him. Ellen Ternan came too, but Dickens did not wake up. He died the next day, lying on the sofa.

Dickens wanted his body to rest in Rochester, a city near Gad's Hill Place, but the British people could not agree to this. He was too important to them.

Dickens died on 9 June, 1870.

Dickens's body was brought to the church in London where the country's most famous writers lie.

Dickens's work became popular around the world. The Russian writers Tolstoy and Dostoevsky both read Dickens. Tolstoy learned English because he wanted to read the novels in Dickens's own language.

Today Dickens is still remembered as one of Britain's greatest writers. His face was on the country's ten pound note for ten years. (It also showed a scene from *Pickwick Papers*.) Dickens was the voice of the country at a time of great change. He had strong opinions and through all his books he tried to make the world better for people. Readers cannot forget the many characters, stories and scenes of his novels. When people think of Victorian England and the conditions in London at that time, many of their ideas are shaped by Dickens's work. His name has even gone into the English language. If a building or place is old and dirty, people sometimes use the word 'Dickensian' to describe it.

Many of Dickens's novels have become stage plays. There have been many TV programmes and films of his work too. From *Oliver Twist* there was a famous theatre show and musical film called *Oliver!* A new film of *Oliver Twist* was made in 2003 by Roman Polanski.

There have been films of *A Christmas Carol* with different actors playing the part of Ebenezer Scrooge. In the 1988 film *Scrooged*, American Bill Murray played a modern Scrooge, not in London but in New York City. Murray gave us a very different kind of Scrooge, but the film's message about Christmas was the same.

And, of course, we still have the books. A few years ago, the British people were asked to choose their favourite books. More than one hundred and thirty years after his death, five of the books in the top one hundred were by Charles Dickens – no other writer, alive or dead, had more books in the list. Dickens's novels are still taught in English literature classes. Readers still grow nervous when Oliver Twist asks for more food. They still get angry when Mr Murdstone sends young David Copperfield to the bottle factory. They still laugh with happiness when Ebenezer Scrooge wakes up on Christmas morning as a new man. In a way, Dickens is still alive through his books. He is still speaking to all his readers.

Bill Murray as Frank Cross, a modern Scrooge, in Scrooged

Talk about it

1 **Work with another student.**

a The year is 1868 and Dickens is in the United States on his last tour of the country. Prepare a list of six questions to ask the writer.

1 ....

2 ....

3 ....

4 ....

5 ....

6 ....

b Now have this conversation.

Student A: You work for an American newspaper. You are going to write about Dickens's life and work. Ask the questions.

Student B: You are Charles Dickens. Answer the newspaper reporter's questions.

2 **Some people called Dickens 'the voice of a nation'.**

a Work with one or two other students. What does Dickens's work tell us about Victorian England? Make notes. Use the Internet if you want to learn more.

b Compare your information with the answers of other groups. Add information to your notes.

56

Plan a Web site for the Internet about Charles Dickens and his work. What will go into it? Write the top page. How can you make it interesting? Possible ideas are:

- facts about Dickens's life
- introductions to two or three of Dickens's novels
- information about your favourite characters from Dickens's novels
- facts about London and England in Dickens's day

1 **Write the titles of three of your favourite books.**

....

....

....

Talk to other students about these books. Explain why you like them. Find one or two students who have read the same book as you.

2 **Work in small groups. Write about an important scene from a book that you have all read. The scene should not have many characters. What happens in the scene?**

A SCENE FROM

....